# Luscious Curves

## Hot Sexy Lingerie & Swimsuit Girls Models Pictures

By **PHOTO ART LOVER**

Copyright © Luscious Curves

All rights reserved. No part of this document may be
Reproduced or transmitted in any form or by any means, electronic, mechanical, photocopying,
Recording, or otherwise, without prior written permission of photo art lover.

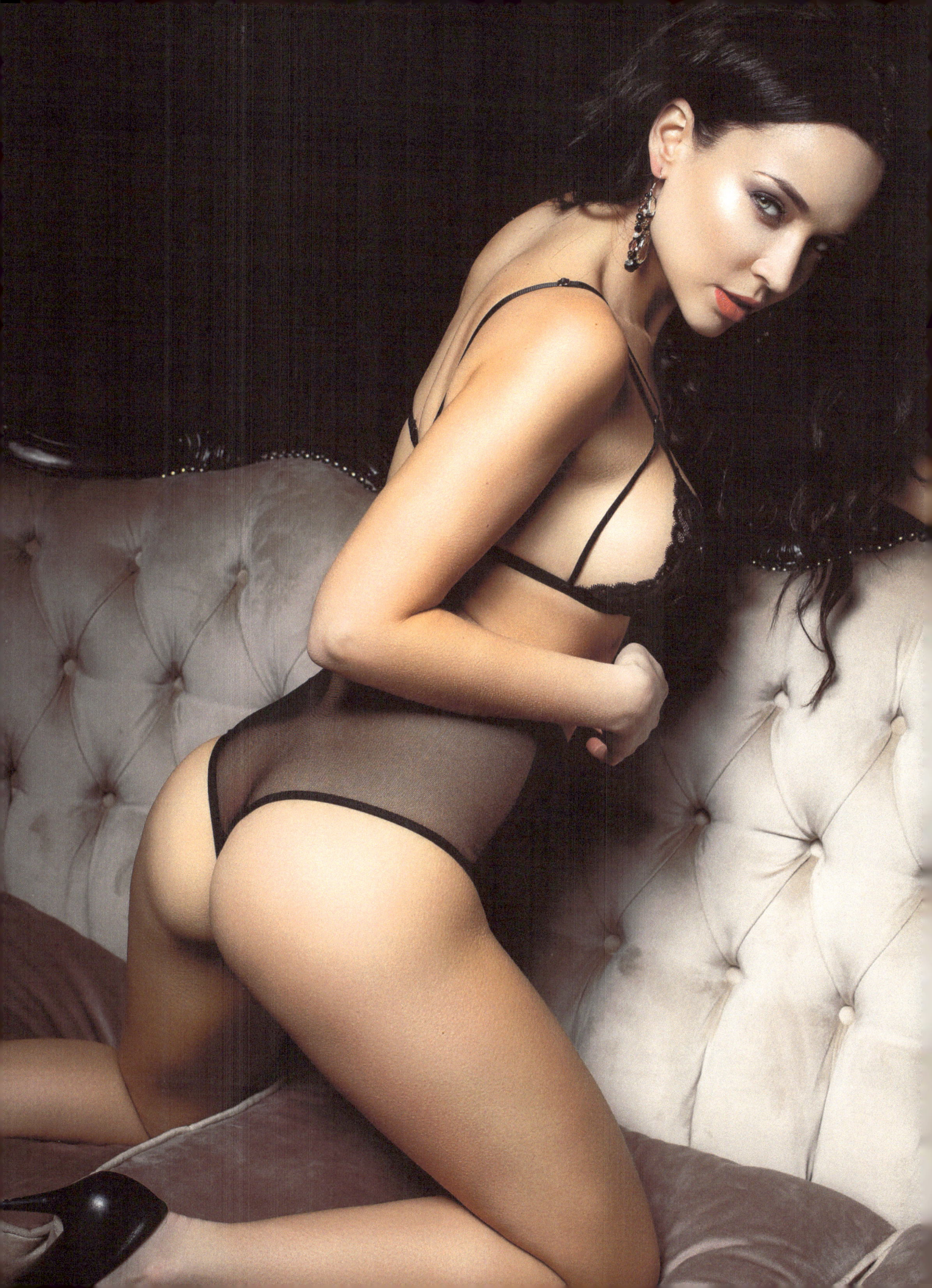

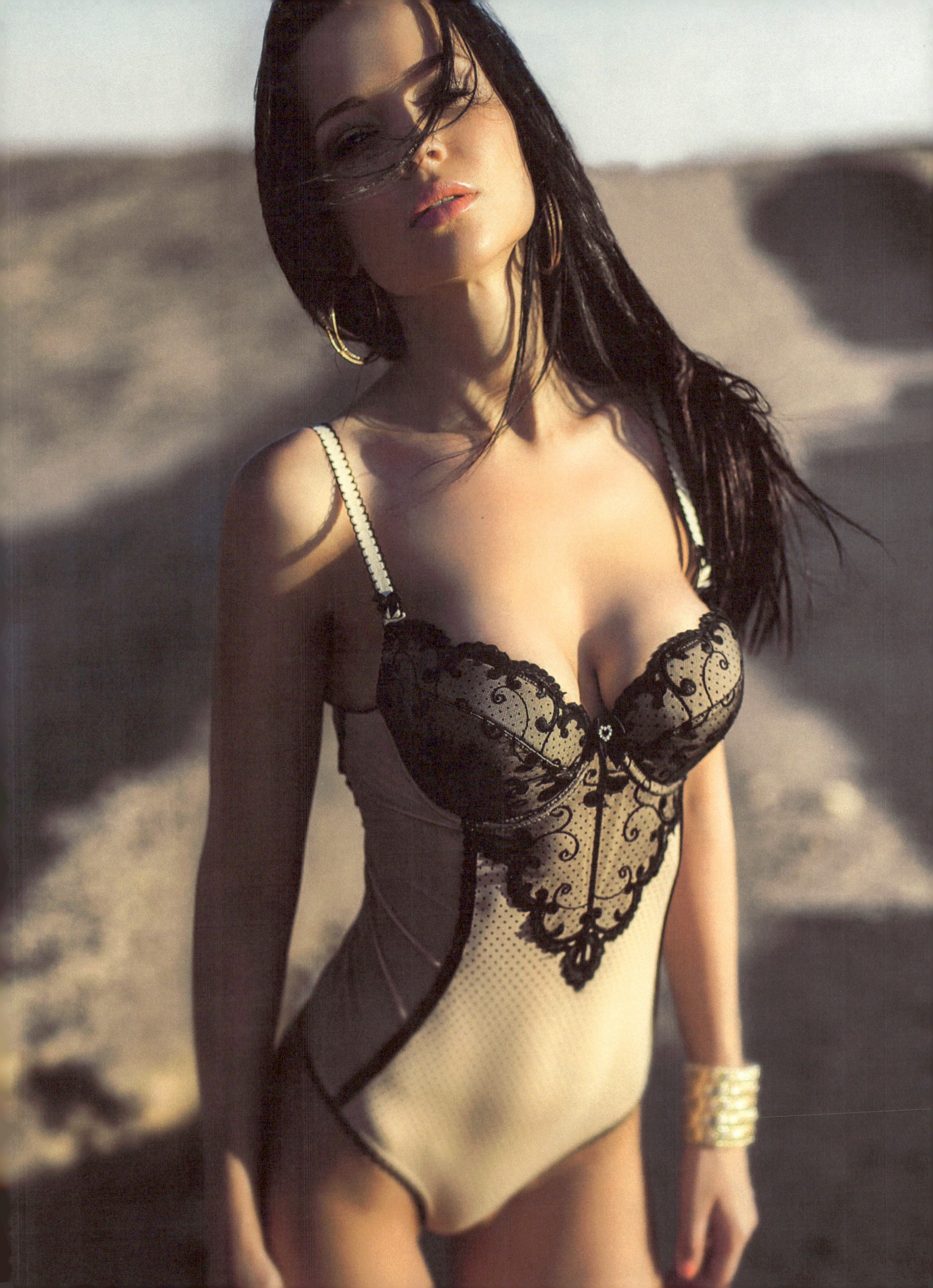

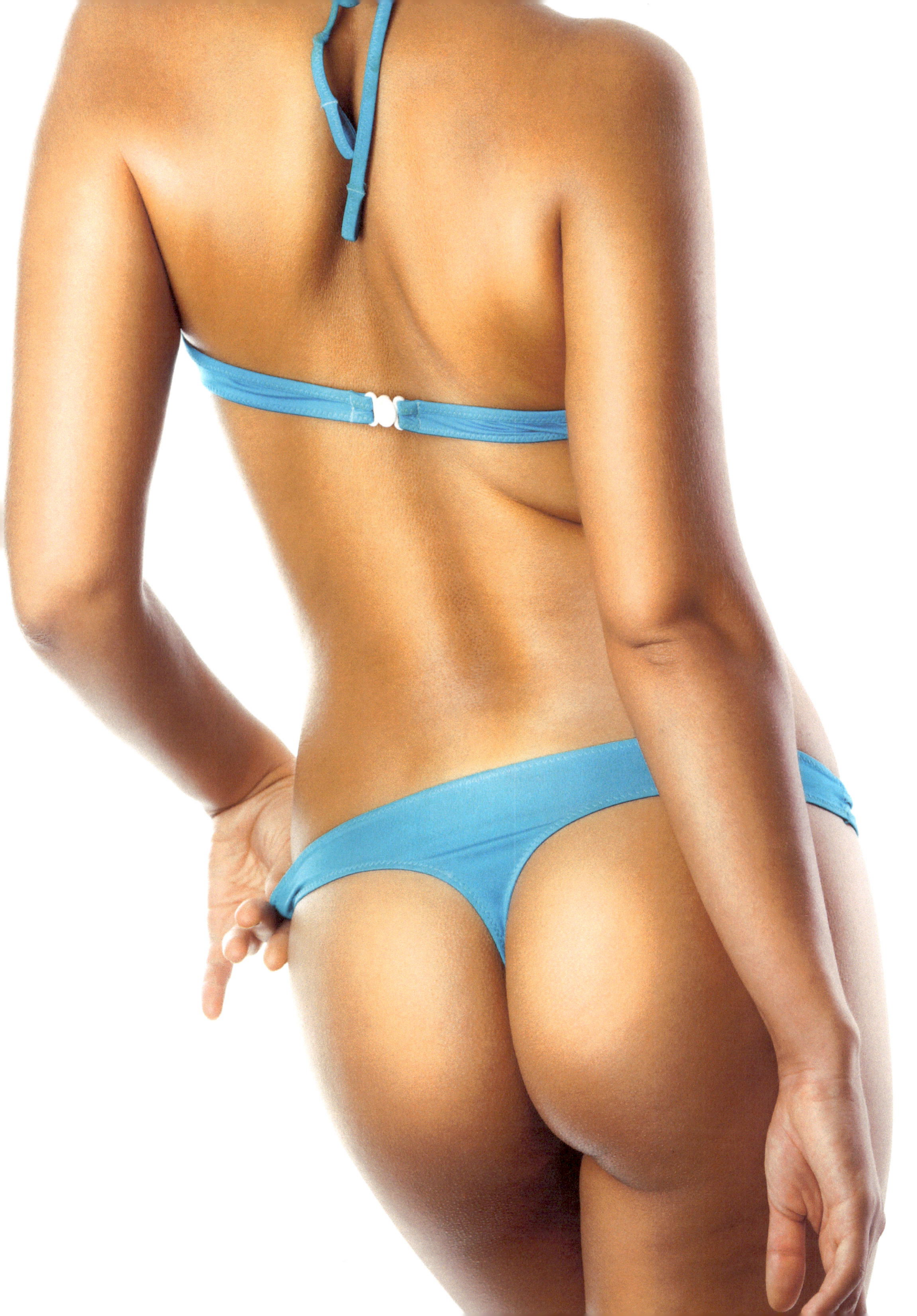

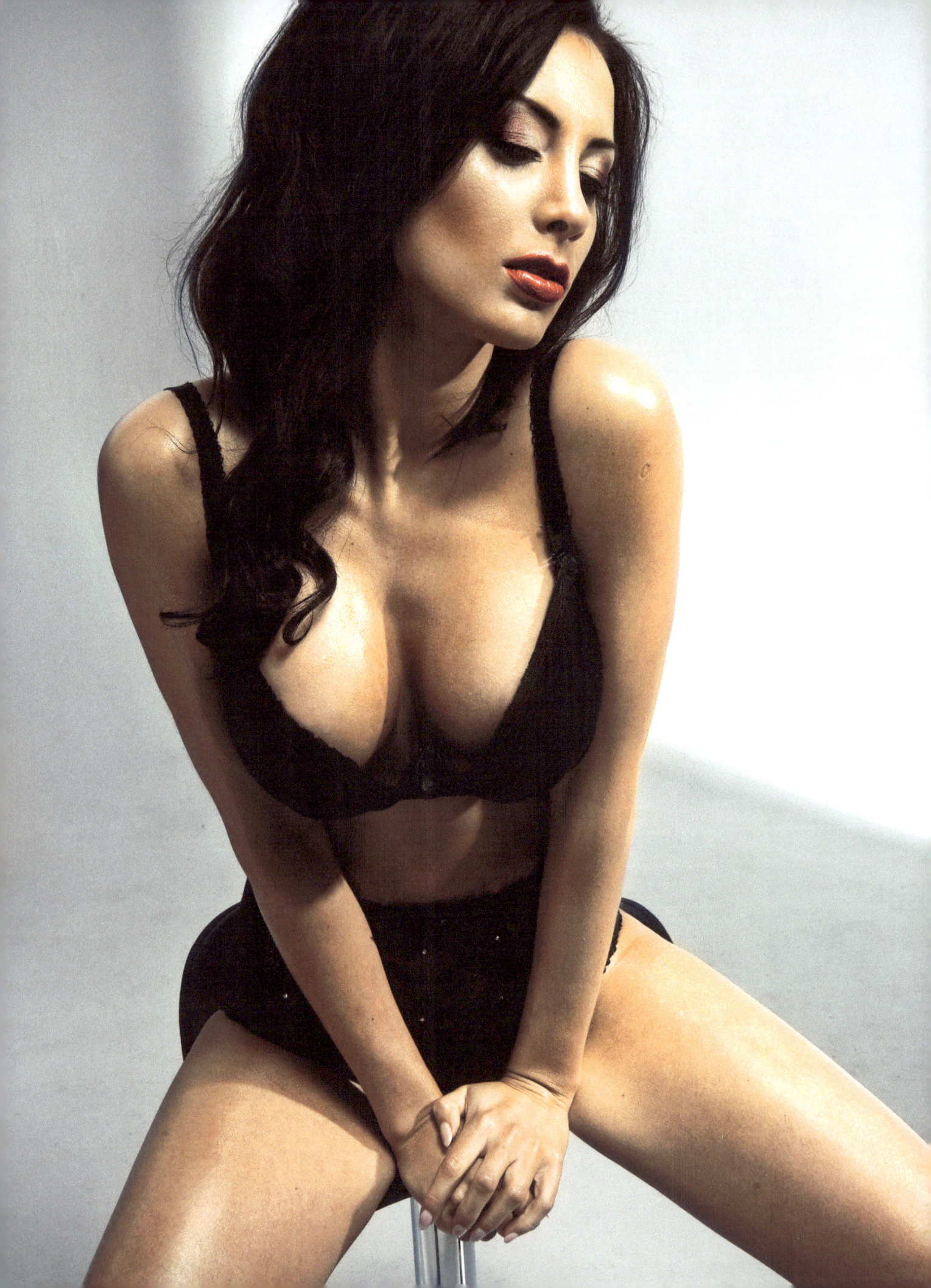

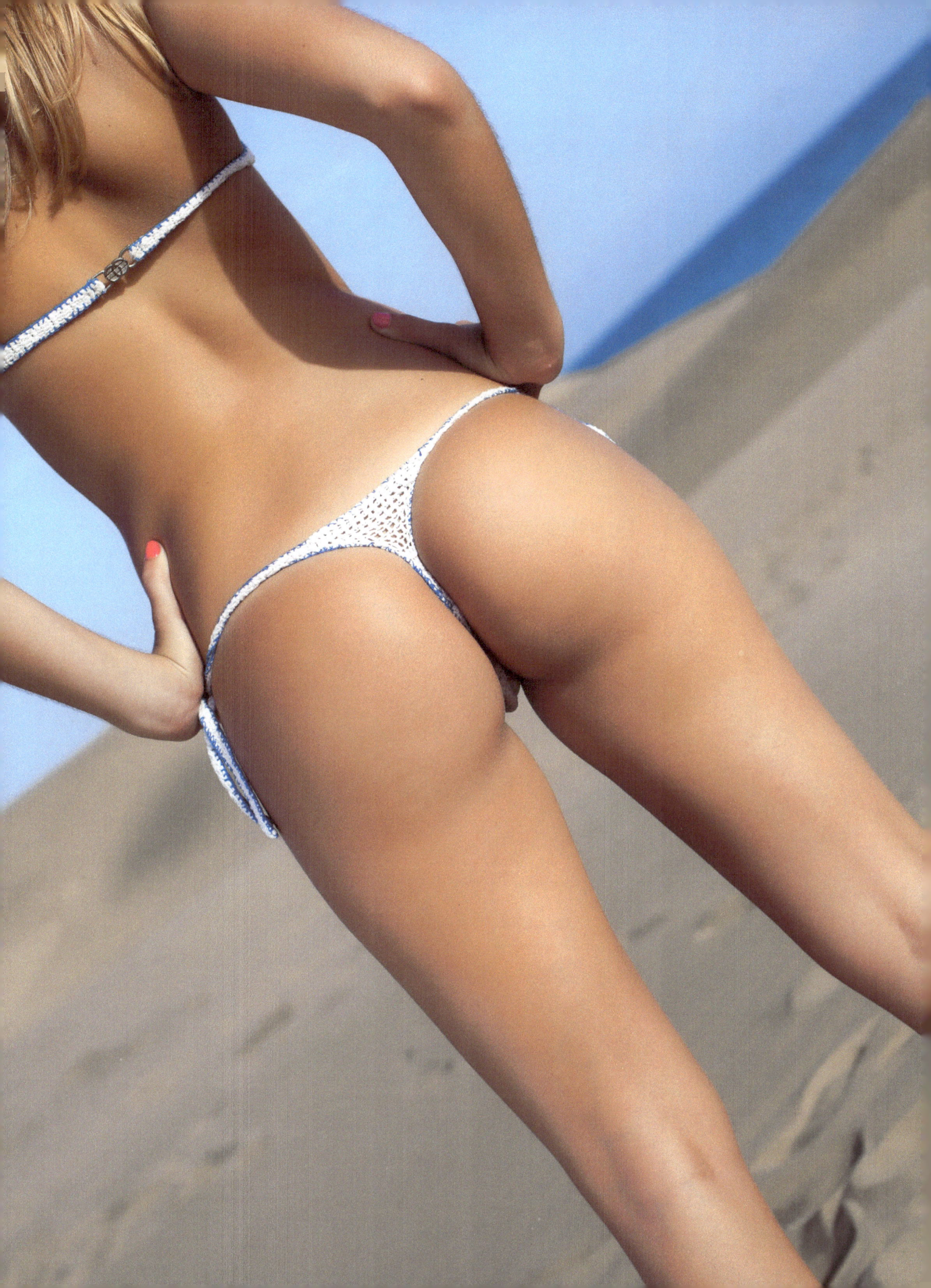

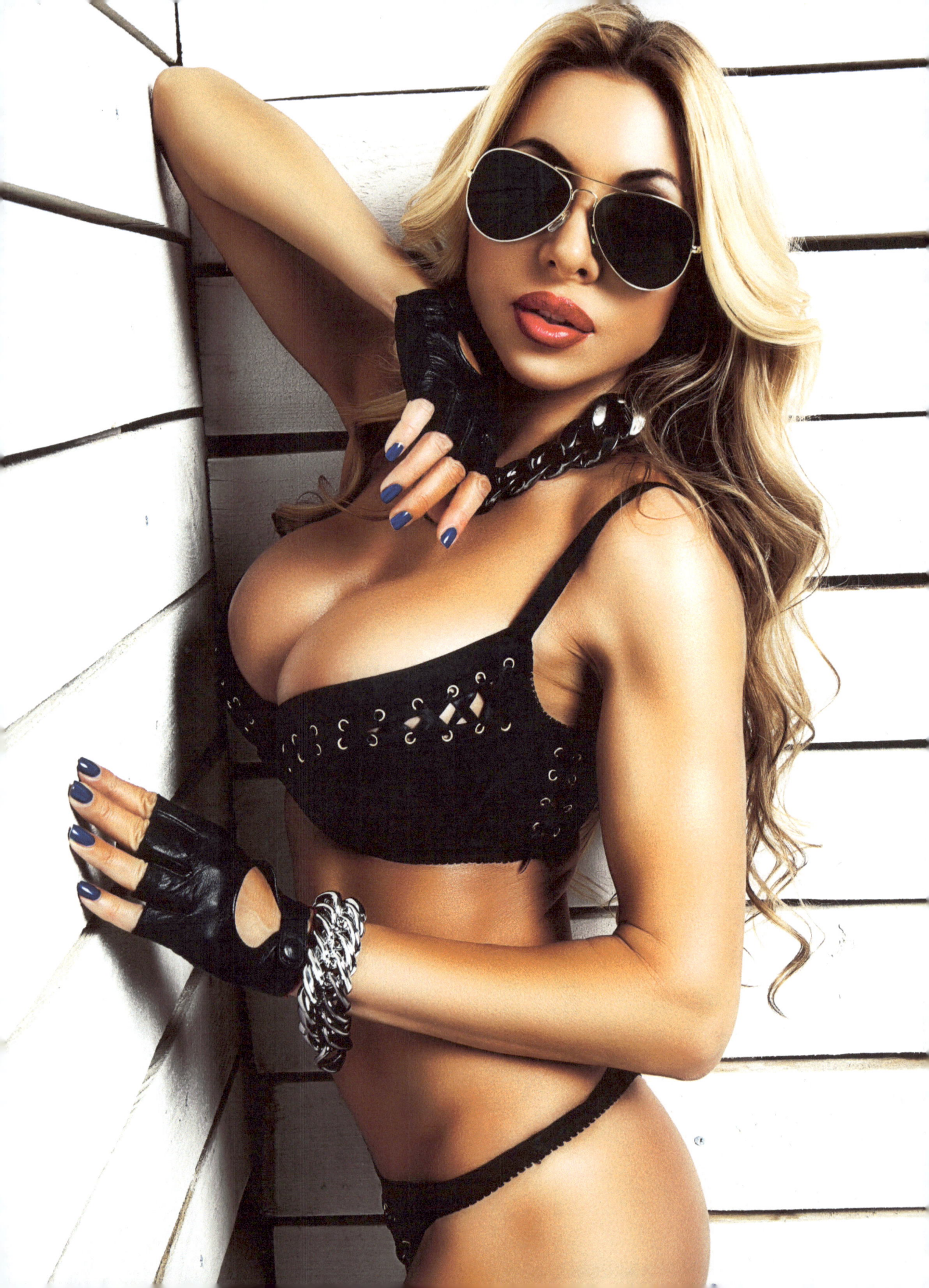

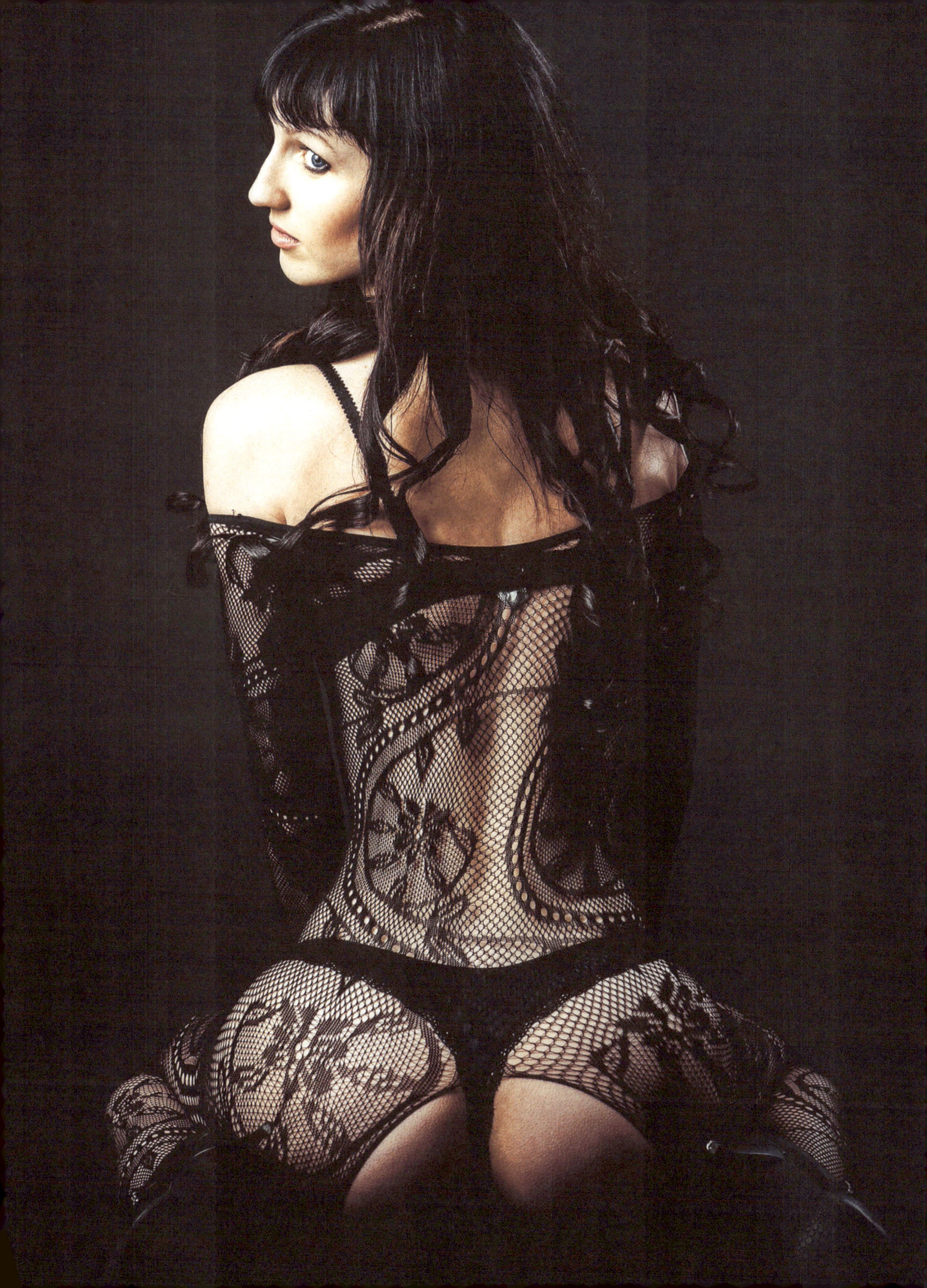

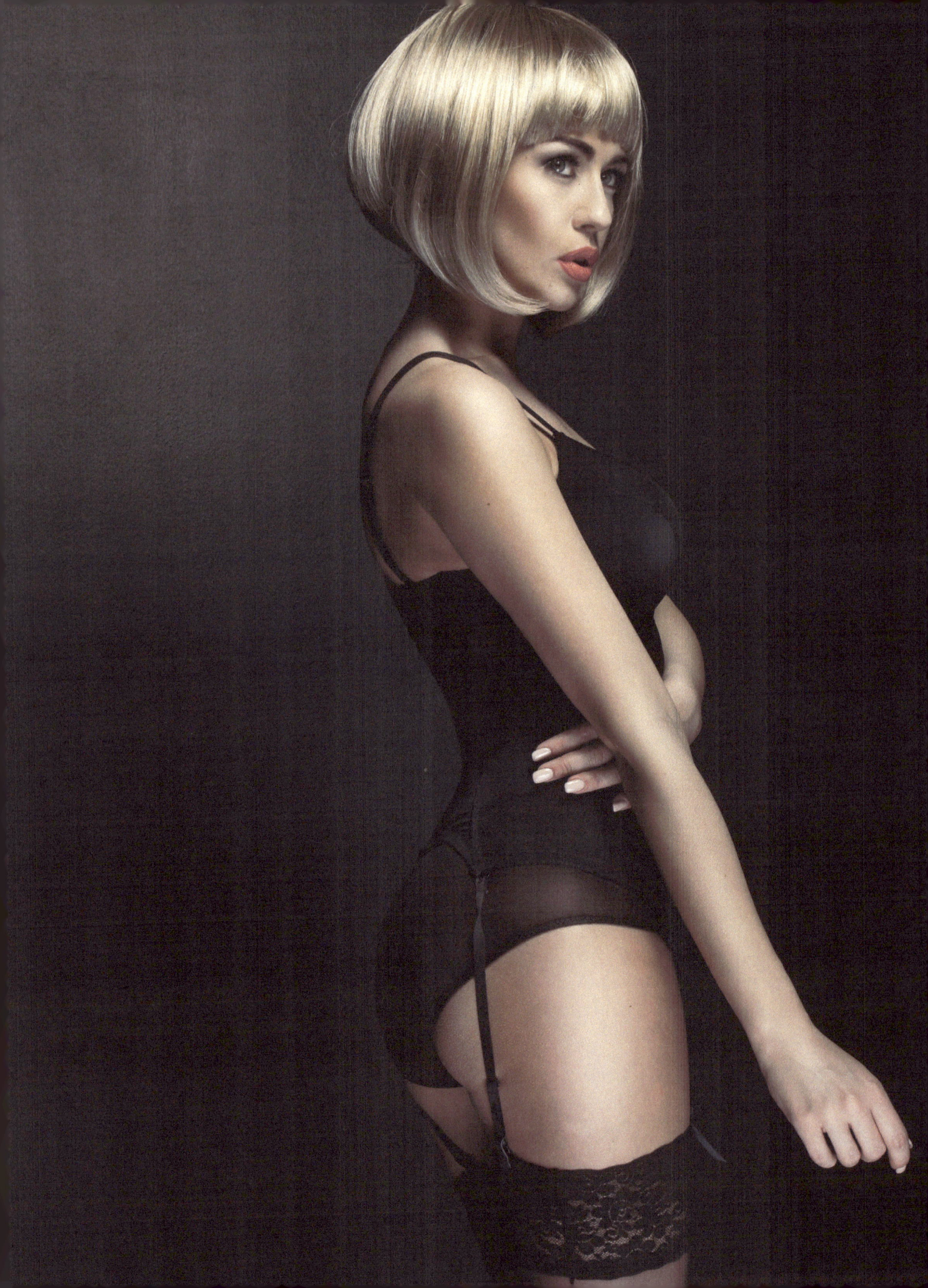

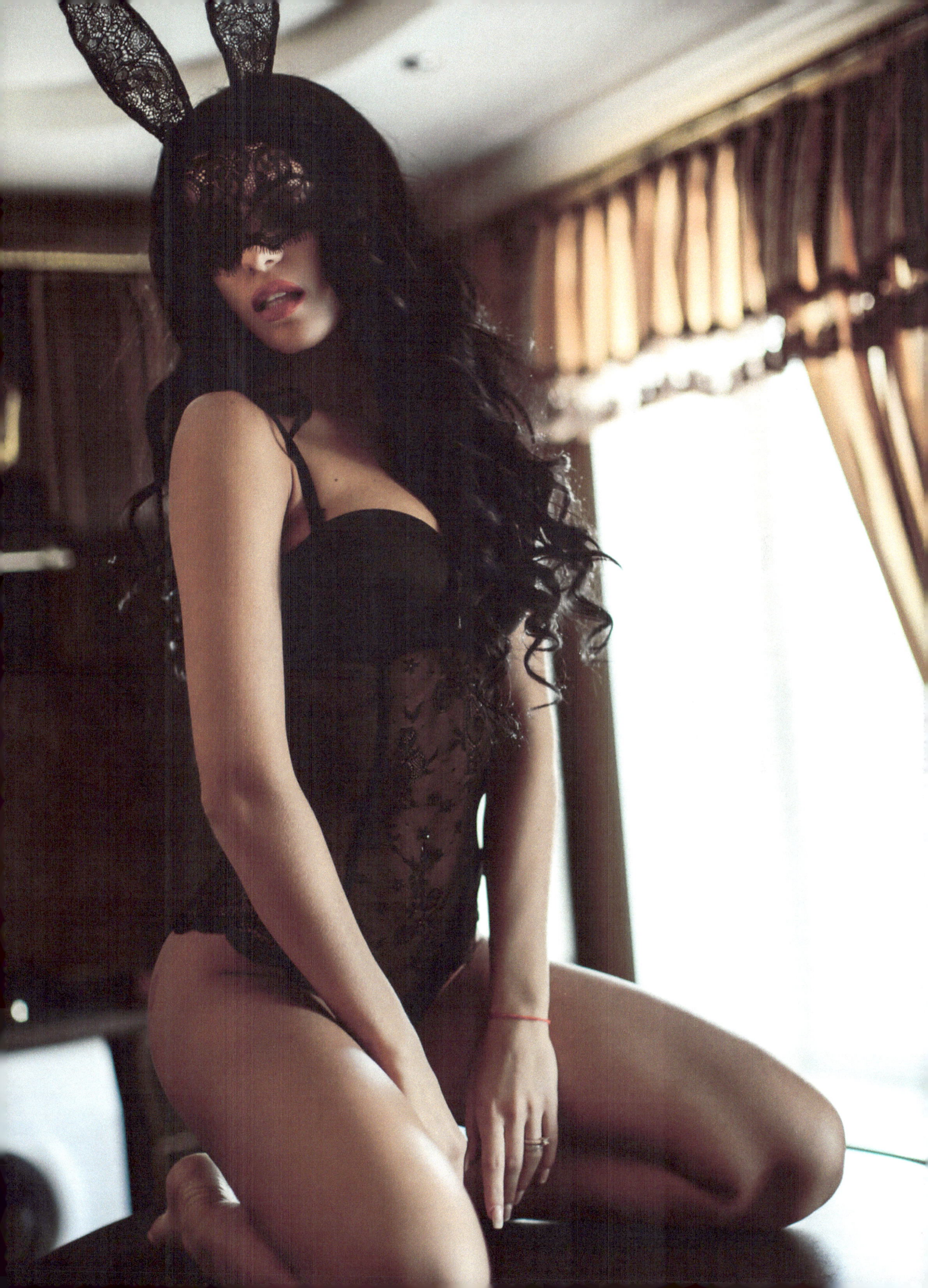

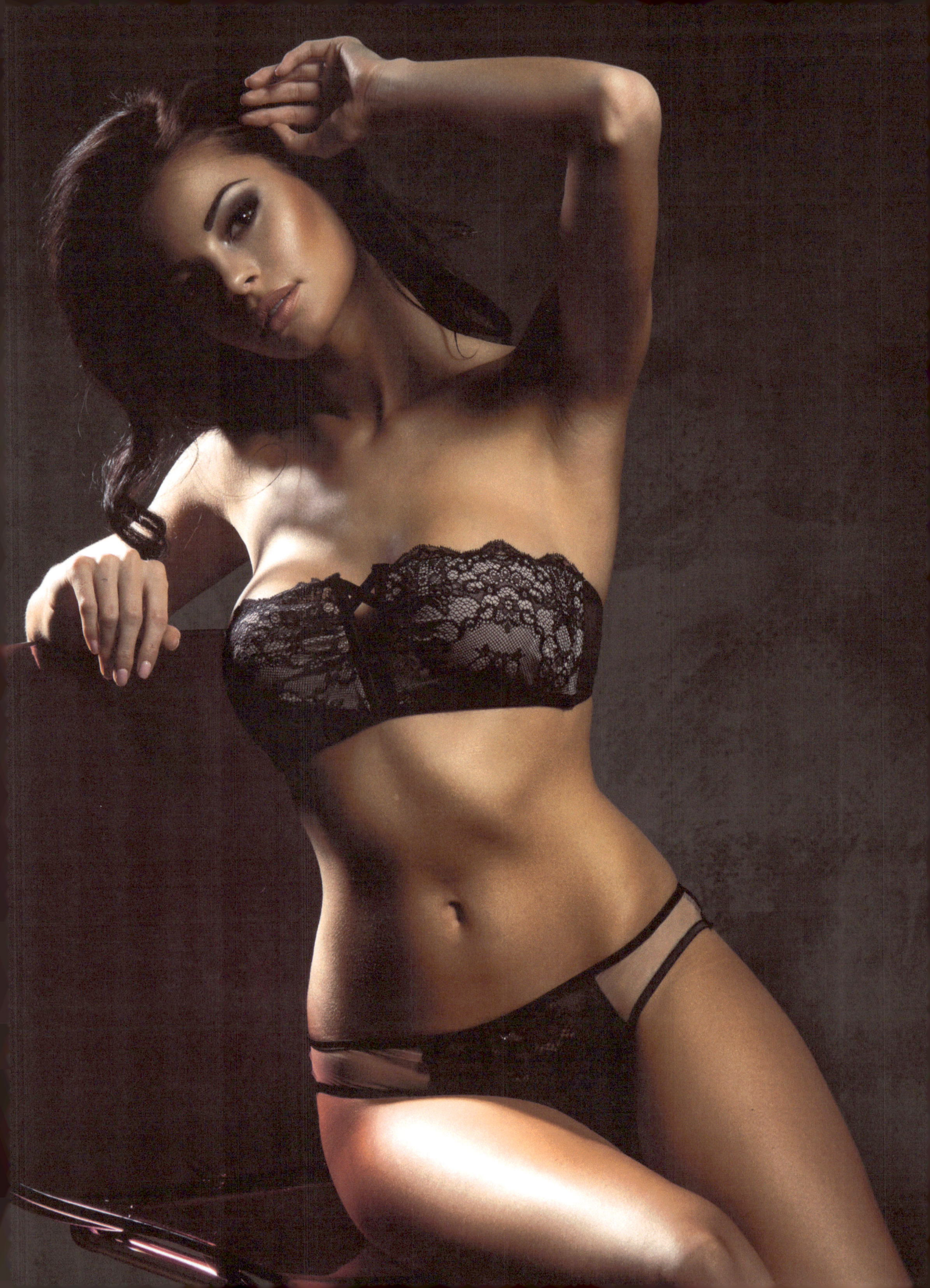

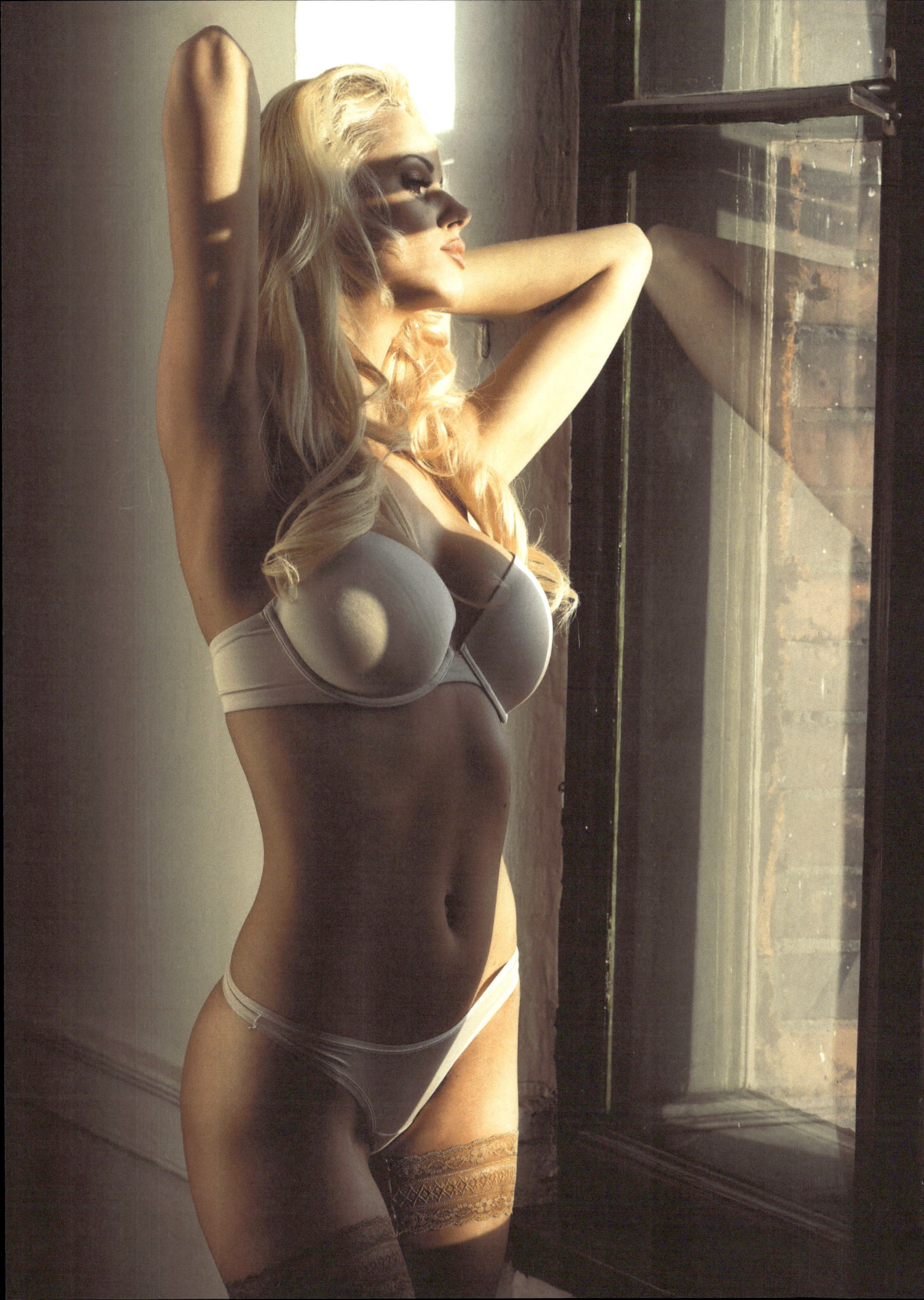

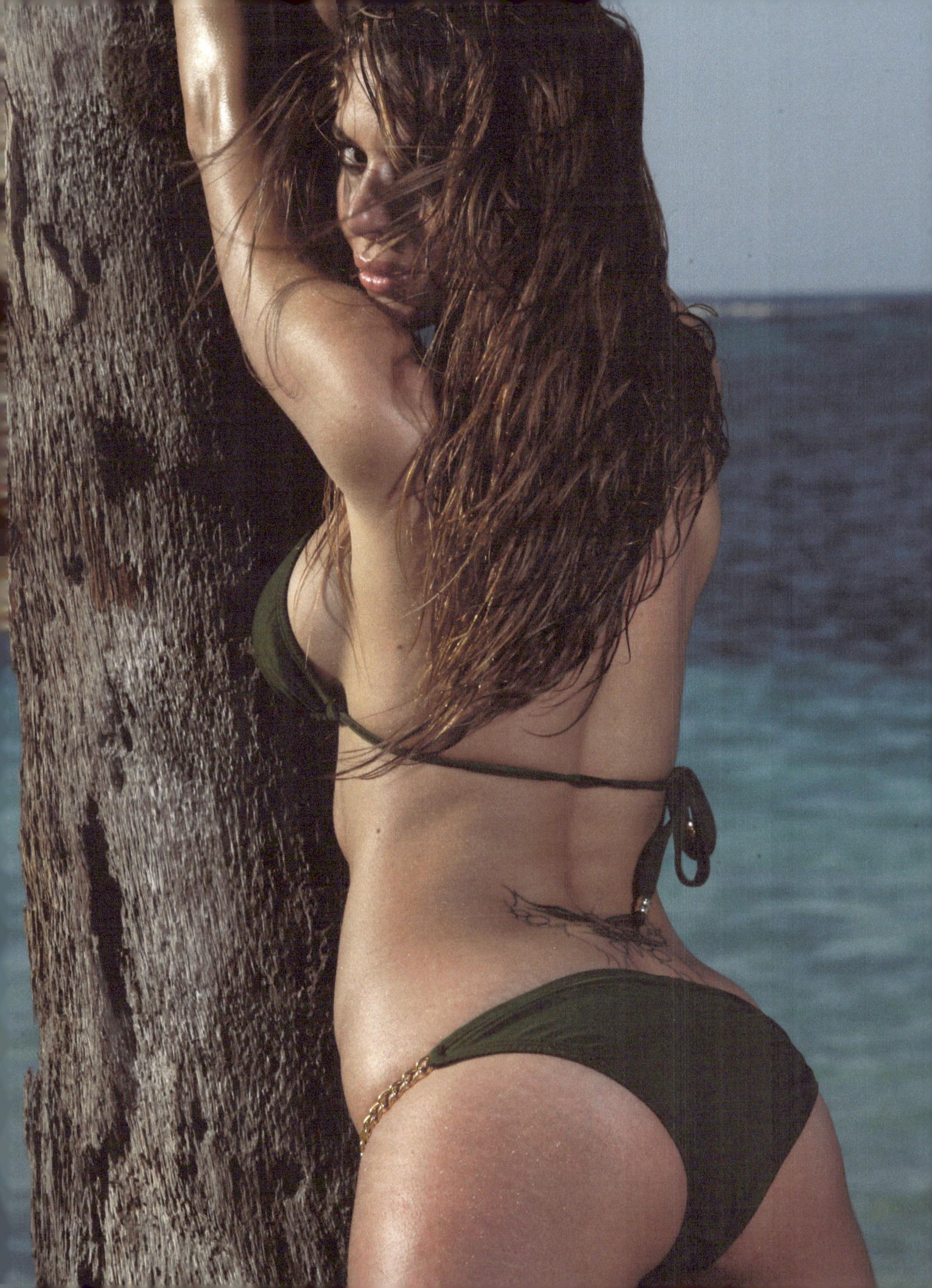

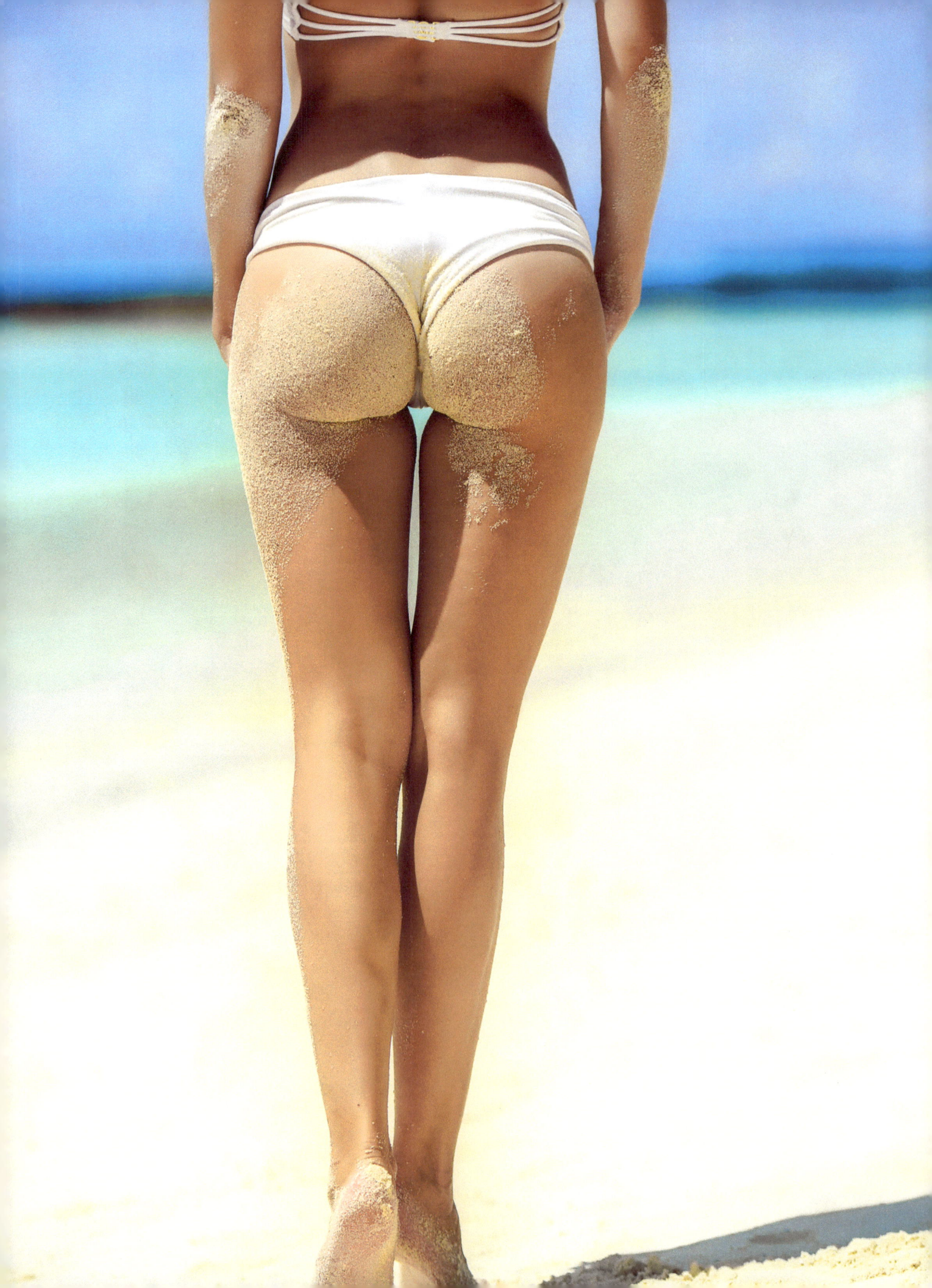

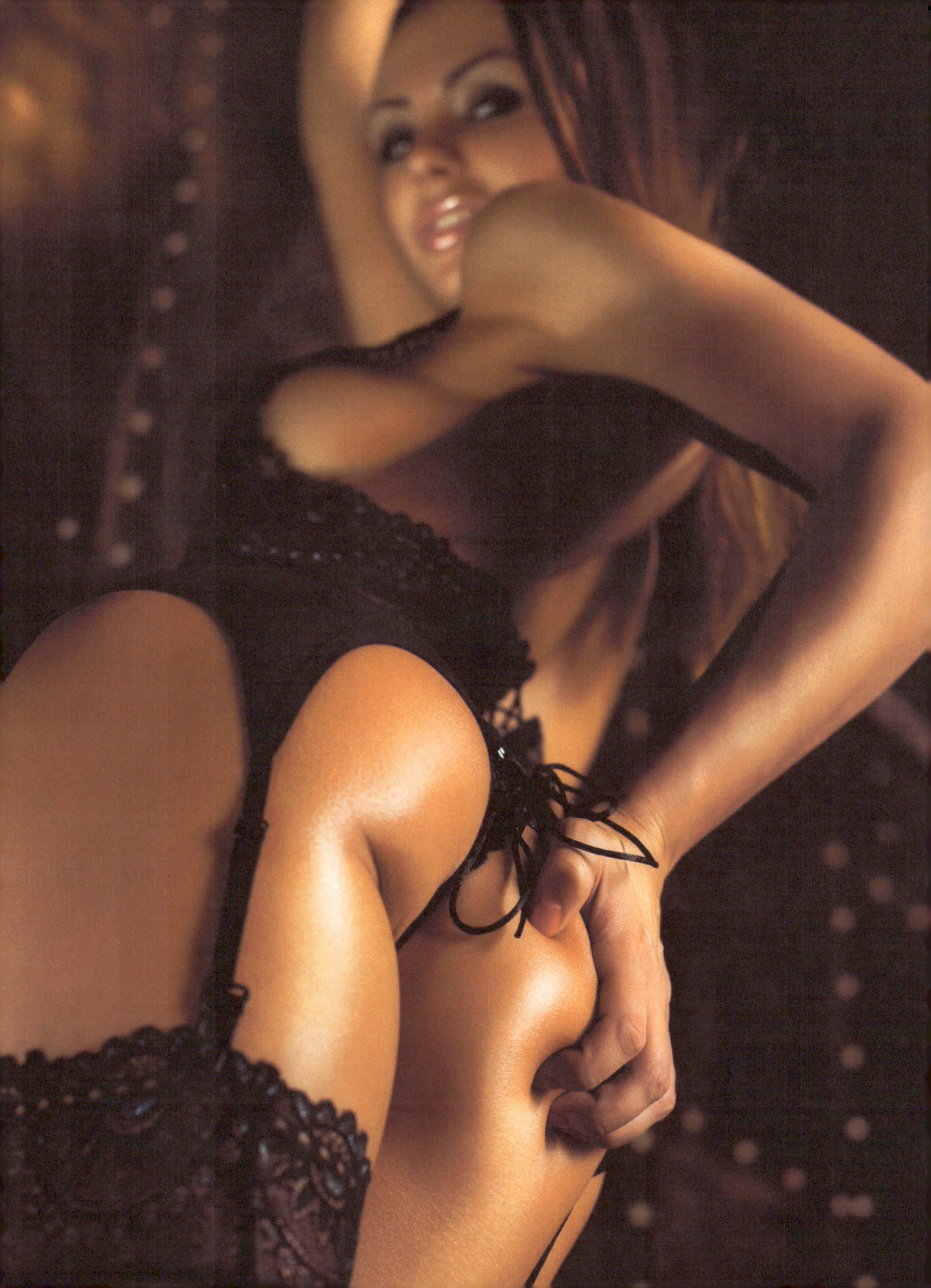

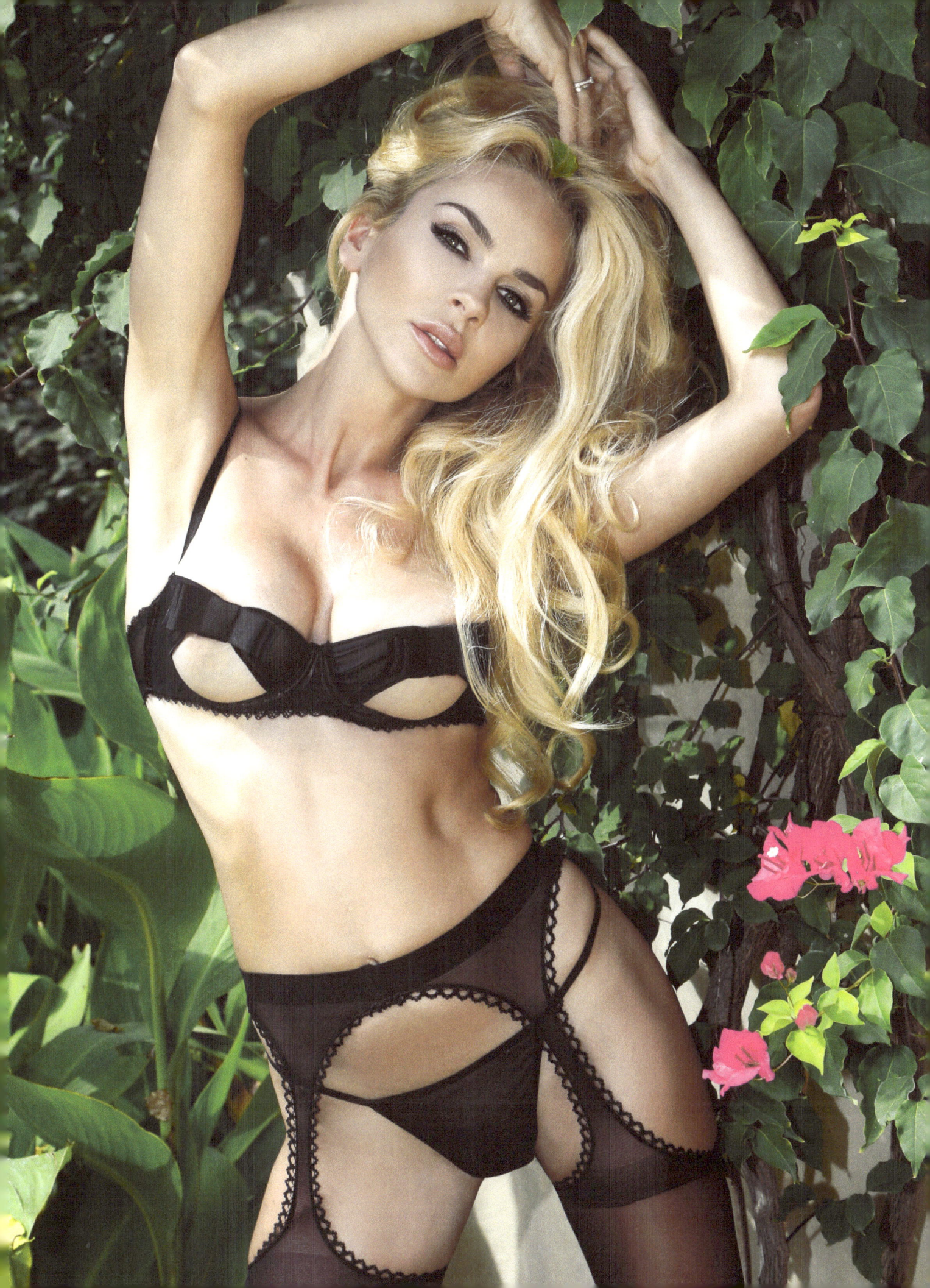

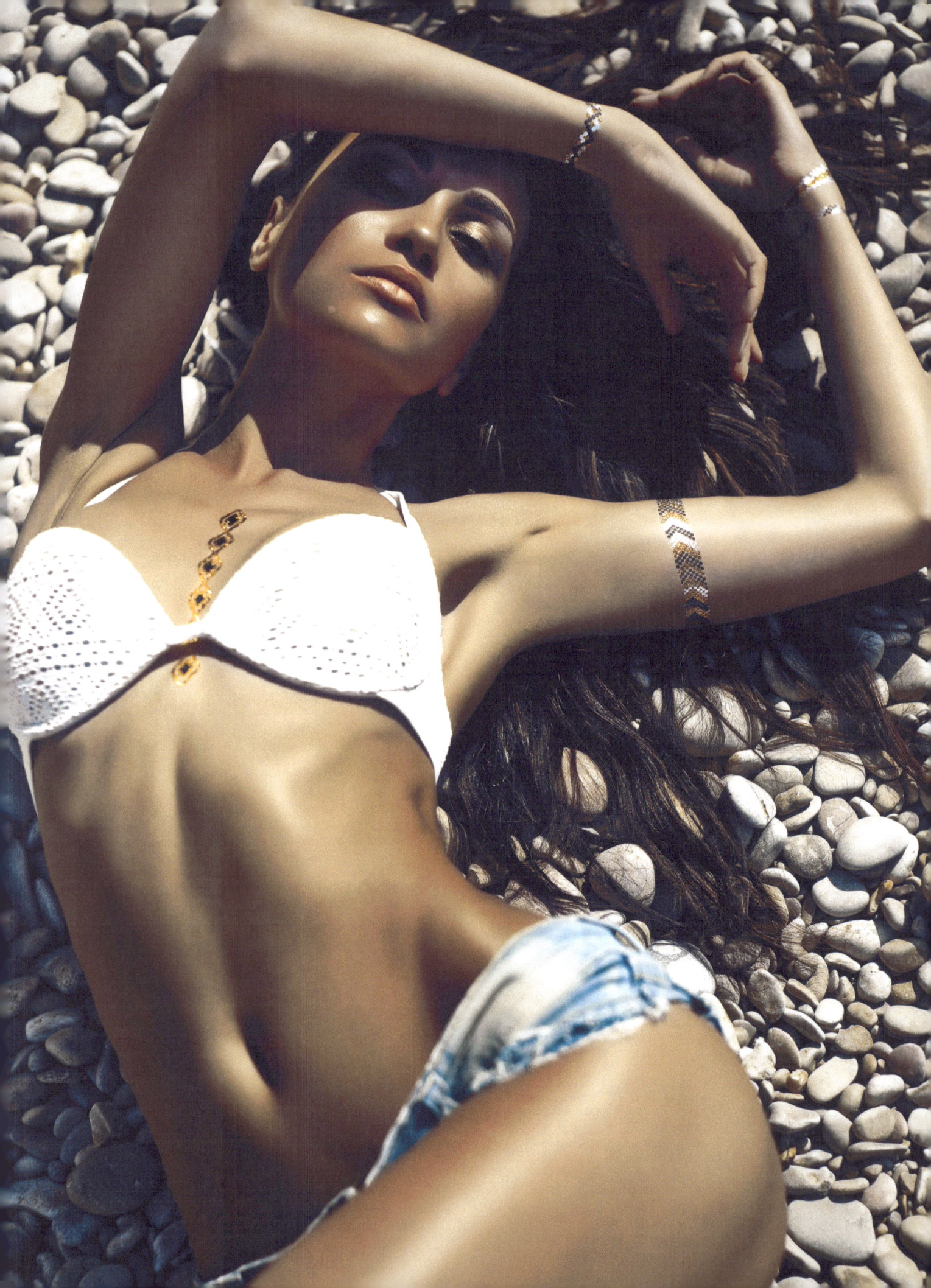

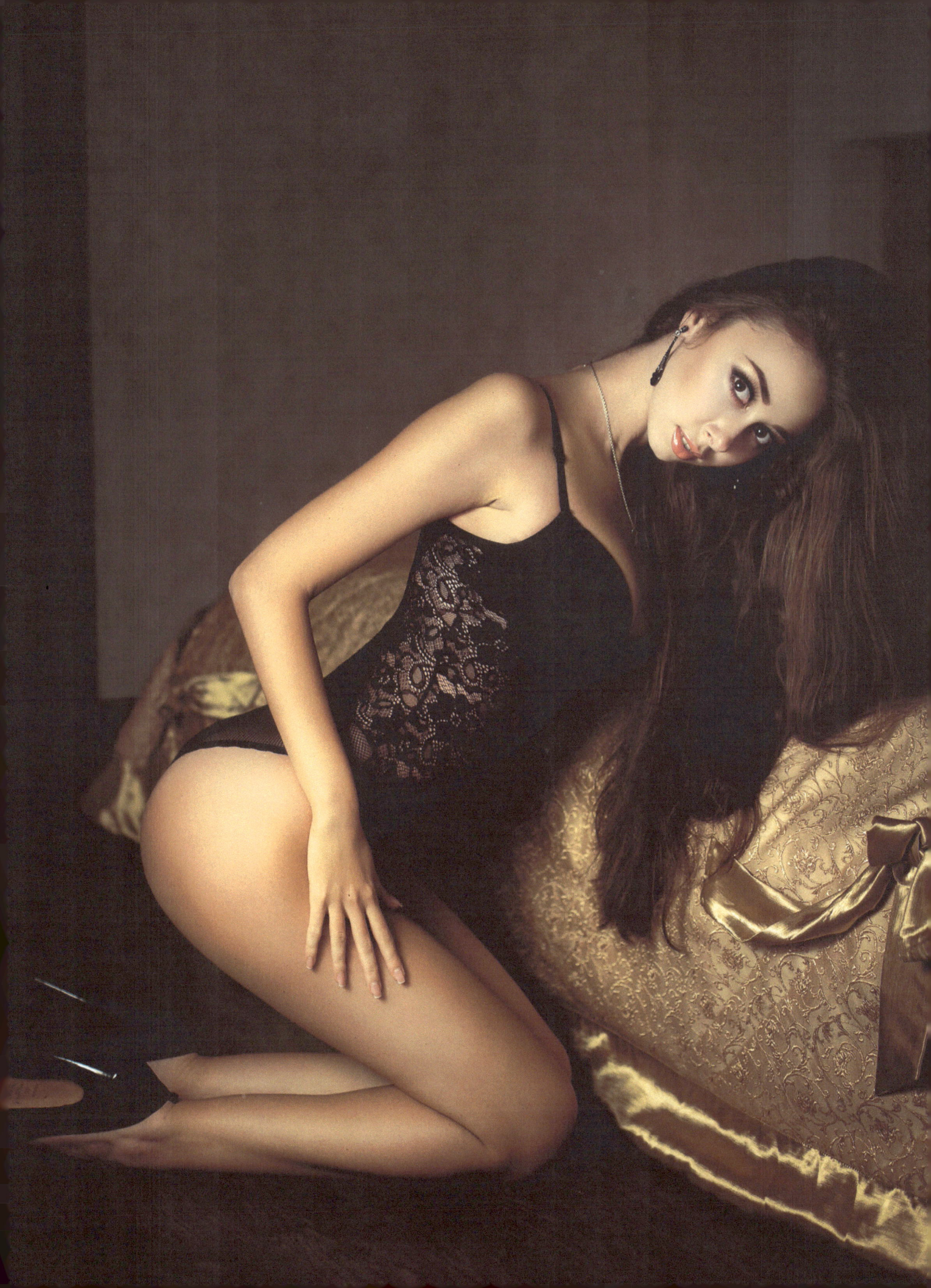

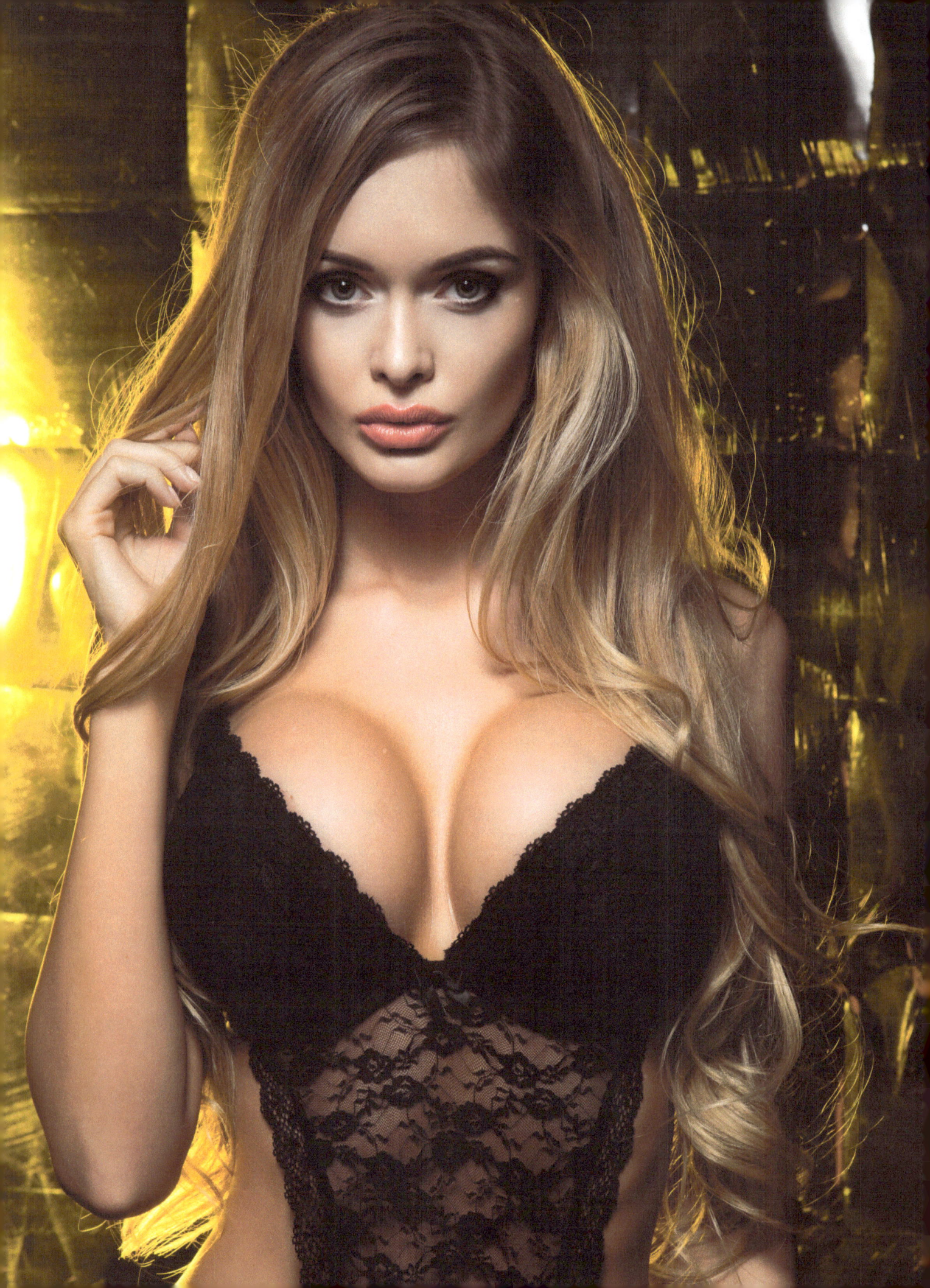

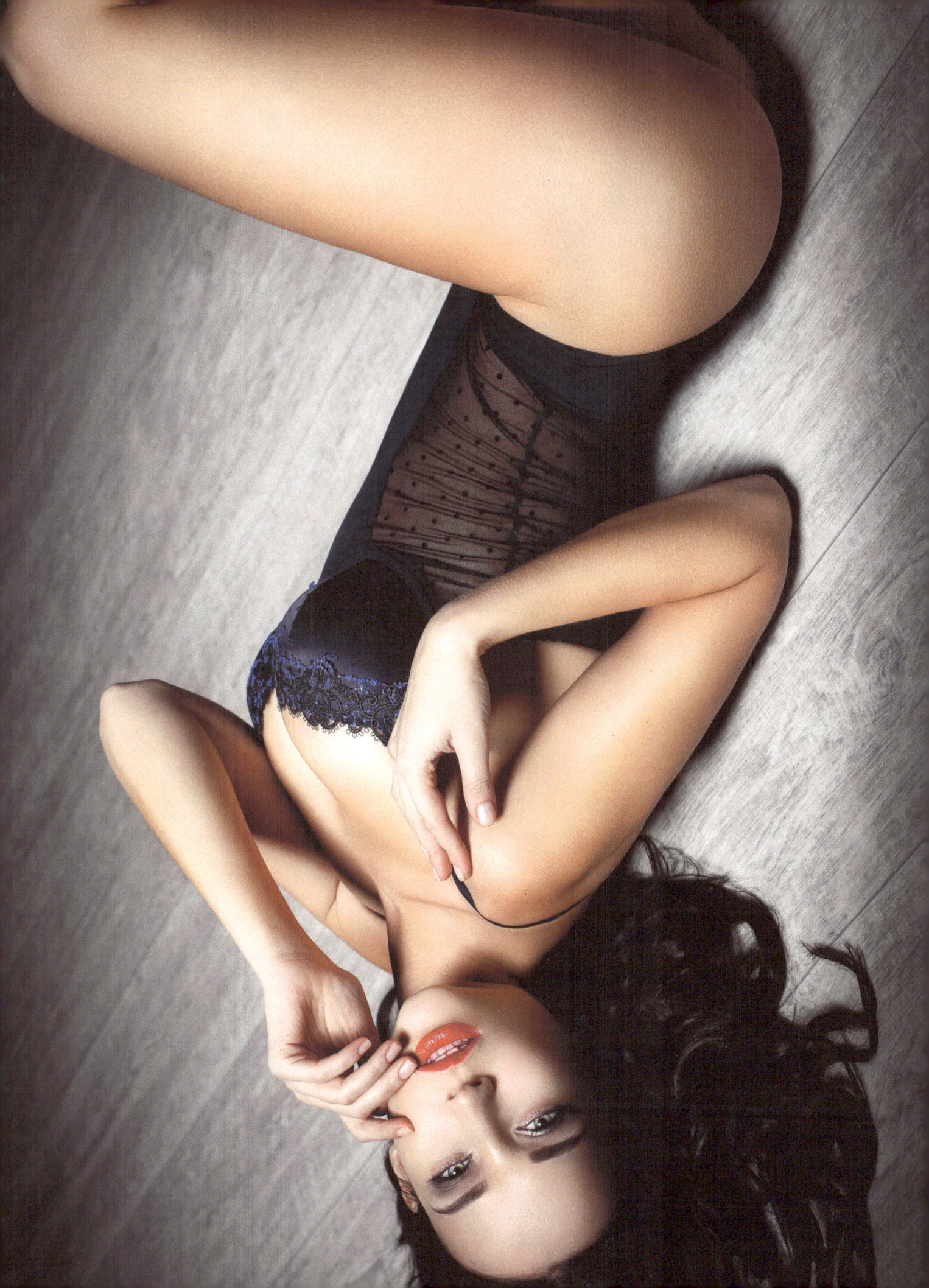

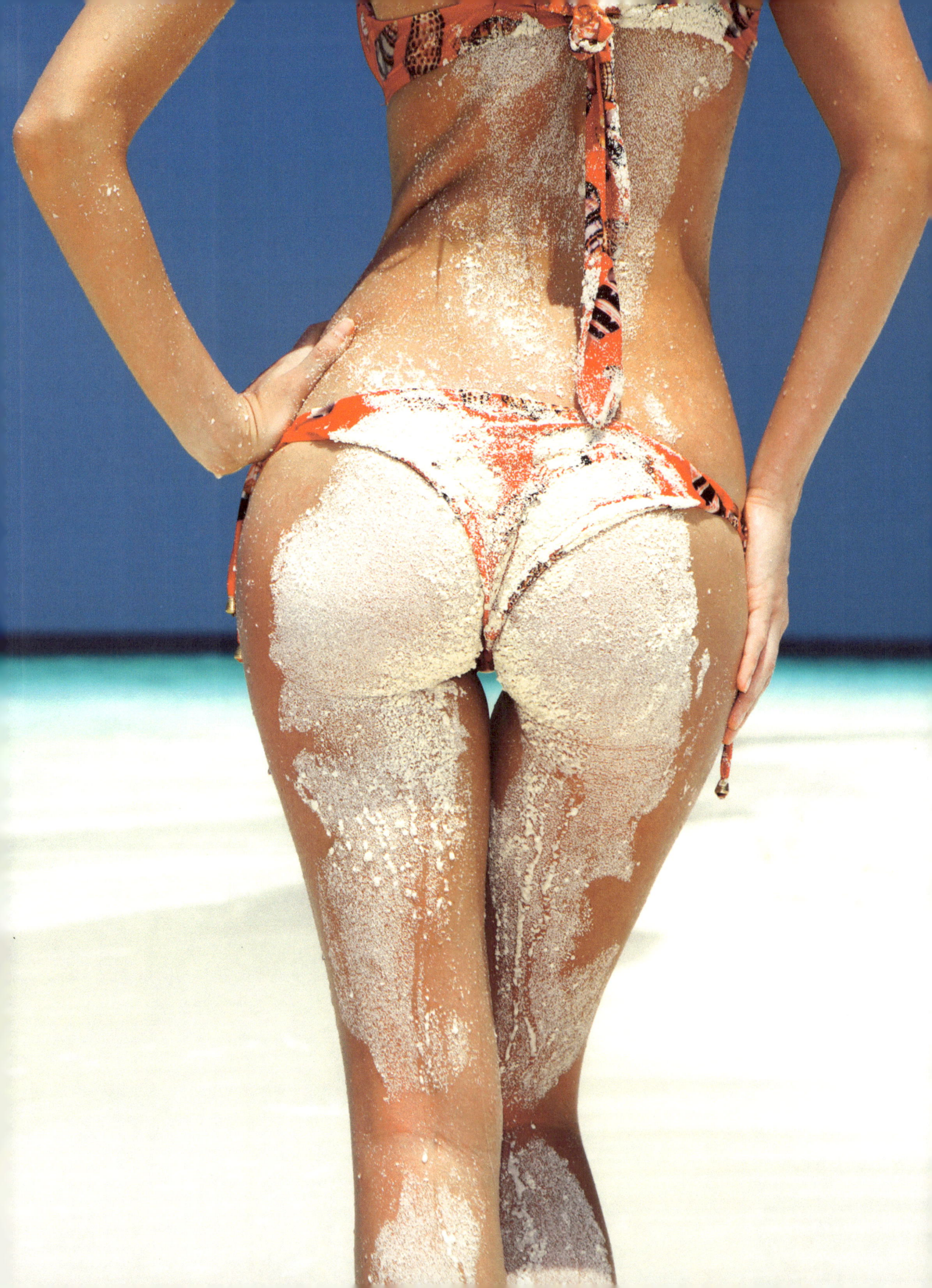

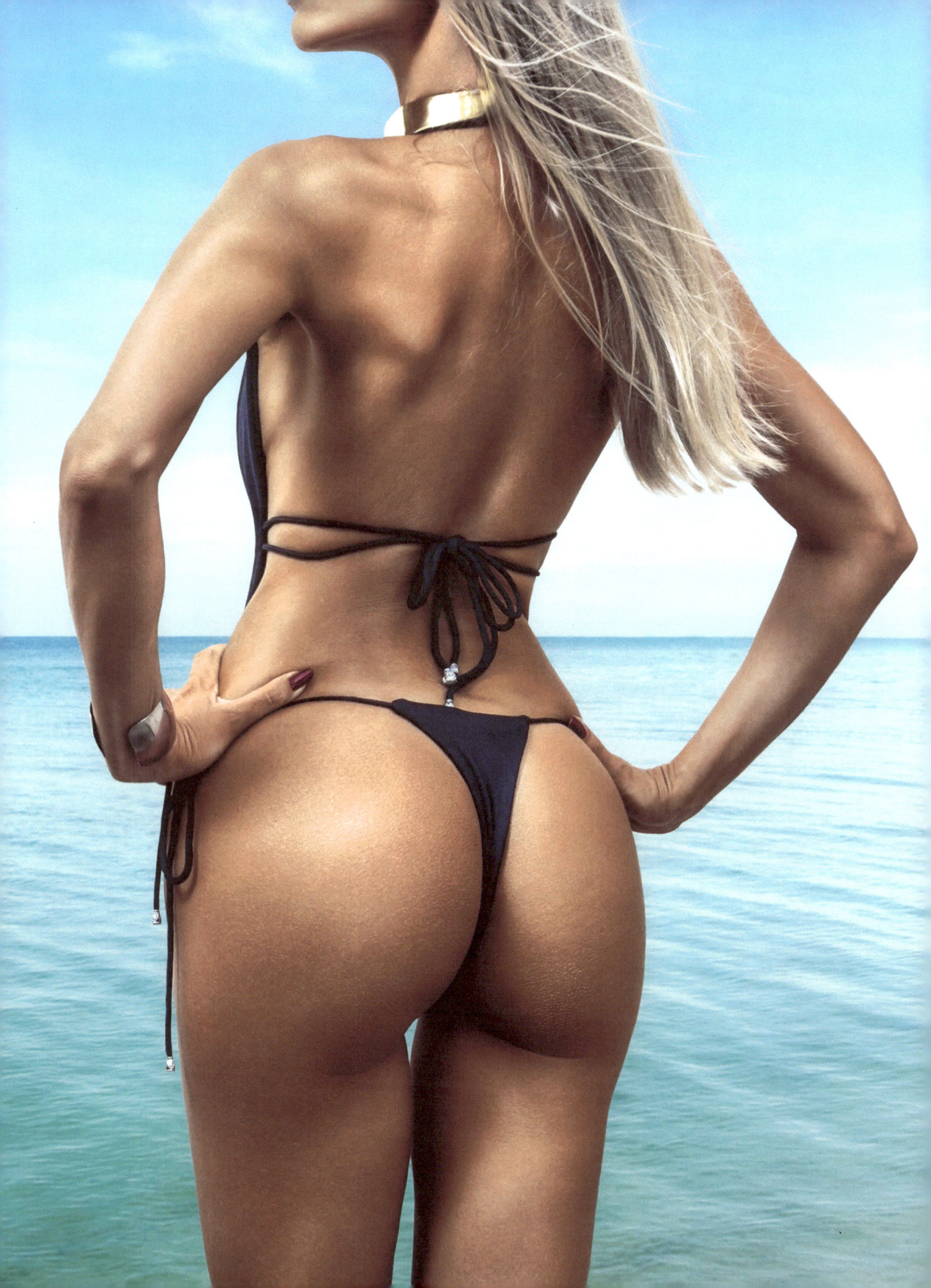

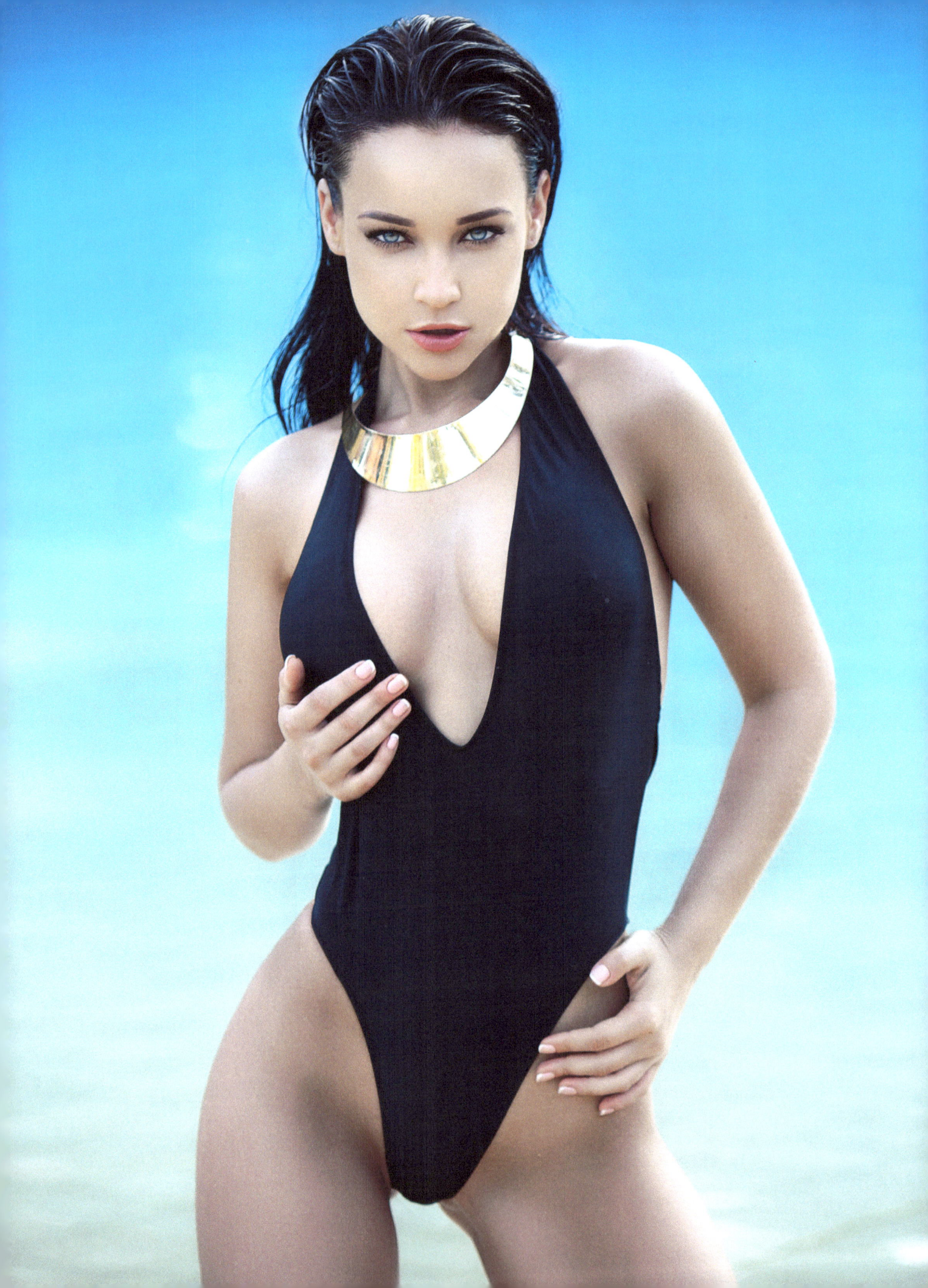

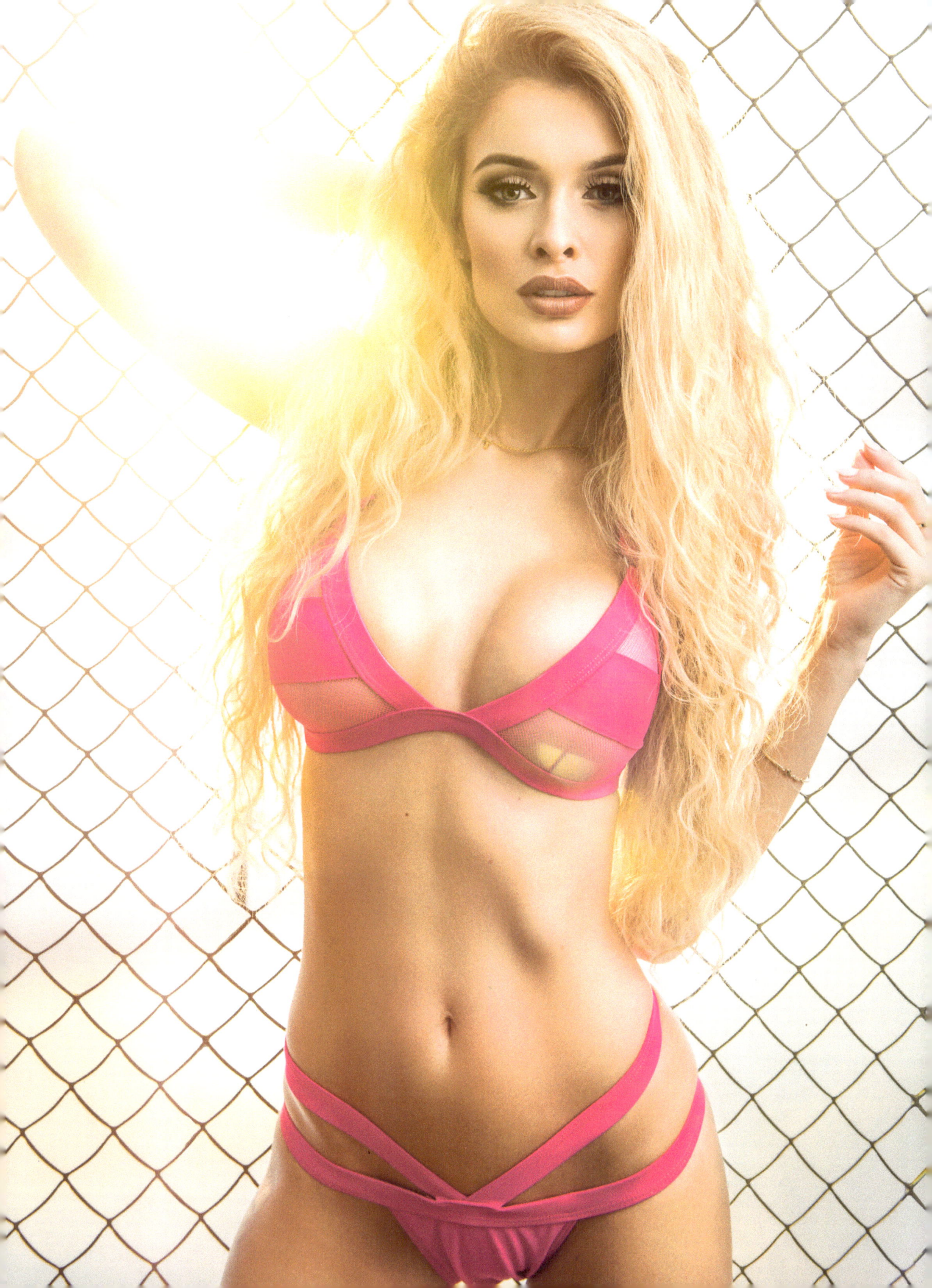

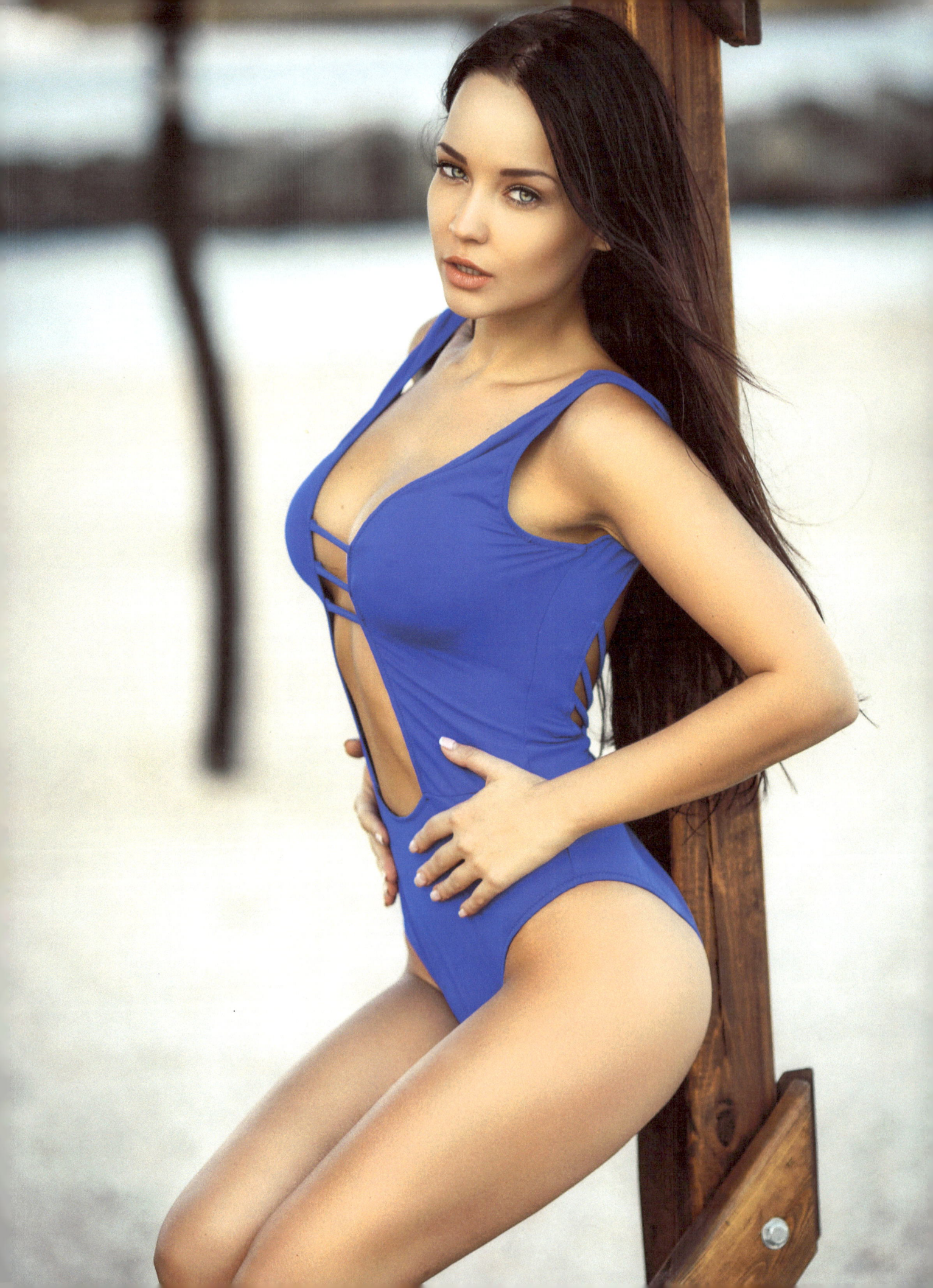

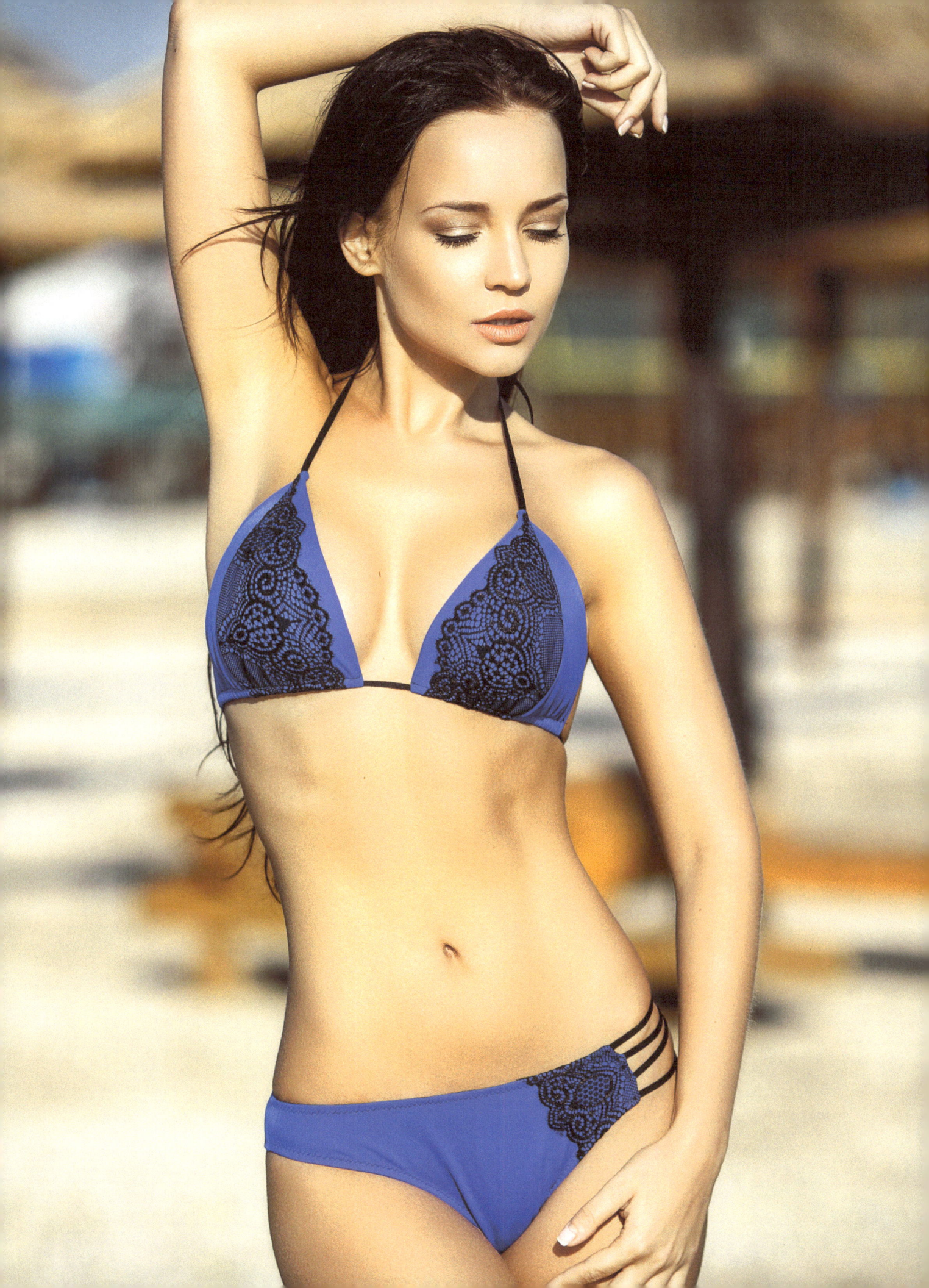

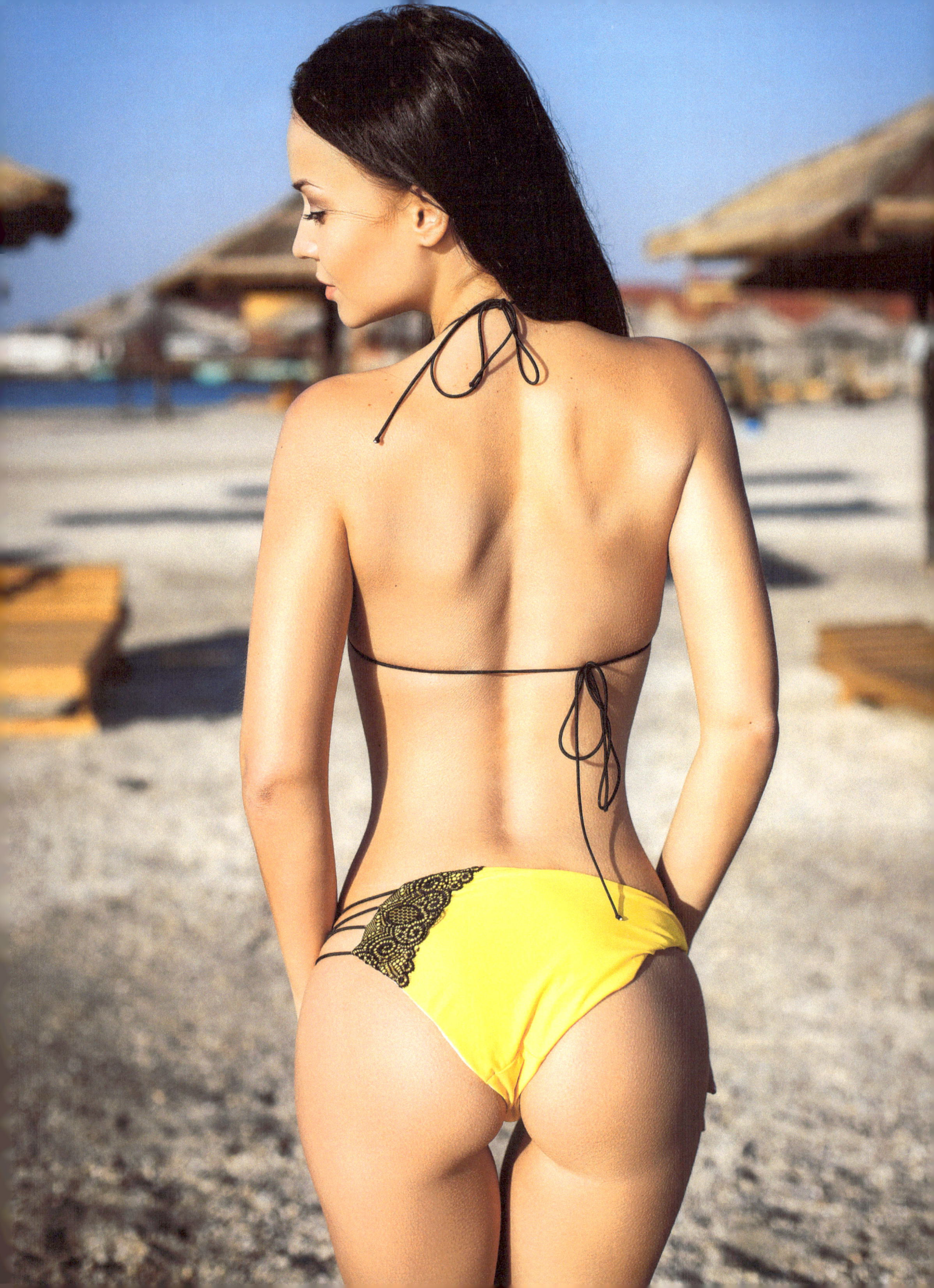

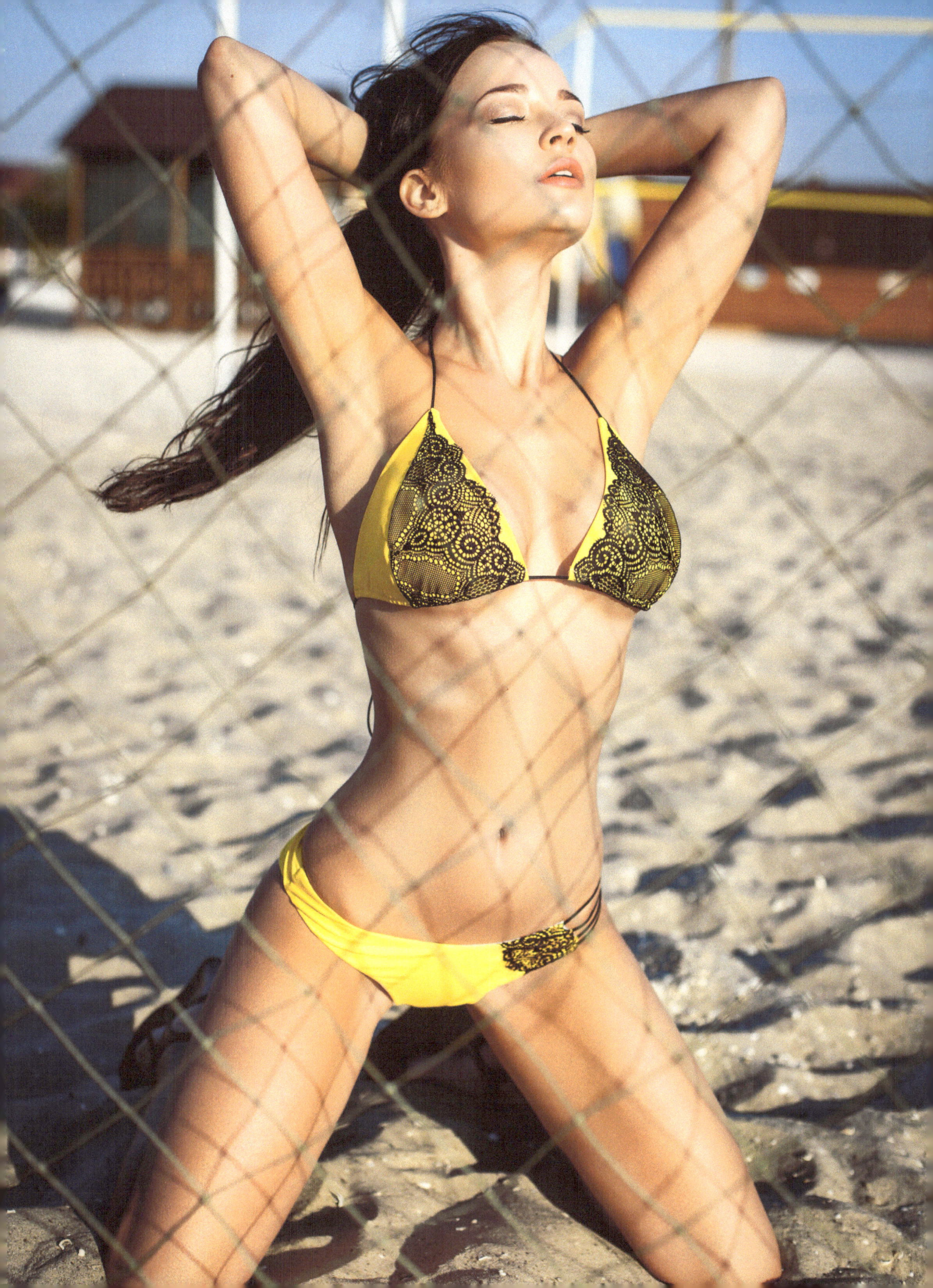

www.ingramcontent.com/pod-product-compliance
Lightning Source LLC
Chambersburg PA
CBHW050420180526
45159CB00005B/2349